CELEBRITY BIOS

Frankie Muniz

Mark Beyer

HIGH
interest
books

Children's Press®
A Division of Scholastic Inc.
New York / Toronto / London / Auckland / Sydney
Mexico City / New Delhi / Hong Kong
Danbury, Connecticut

Book Design: Laura Stein
Contributing Editor: Matthew Pitt

Library of Congress Cataloging-in-Publication Data

Beyer, Mark (Mark T.)
    Frankie Muniz / Mark Beyer.
        p. cm. — (Celebrity bios)
    Includes biographical references and index.
    Summary: Profiles the actor who stars in the television series,
    "Malcolm in the Middle," focusing on how he turned an interest
    in theater into a career.
        ISBN 0-516-23910-4 (lib. bdg.) — ISBN 0-516-23480-3 (pbk.)
        1. Muniz, Frankie, 1985—-Juvenile literature. 2. Actors—United
    States—Biography—Juvenile literature. [1. Muniz, Frankie, 1985– 2.
    Actors and actresses.] I. Title. II Series

    PN2287 .M795 B49 2002
    791.45'028'092—dc21
    [B]
                                                2001037277

CONTENTS

CHAPTER ONE

THUMBS UP!

"With acting, you never know what's going to happen!"

—Frankie Muniz in an *AT&T WorldNet Online* interview

Frankie Muniz walked out of the biggest audition of his life with a frown. It was 1999, and he was trying out for the part of Malcolm in "Malcolm in the Middle." He was sure he'd get turned down. Malcolm was supposed to be nine years old. Frankie was thirteen. It didn't

Frankie Muniz hitched an early ride to stardom.

5

matter to him that he looked young for his age. A nine-year-old was too young for him to play, he thought. He spotted his mom and gave her a quick signal: thumbs down.

Lucky for Frankie, the producers of the Fox show saw his audition tape differently. As soon as they watched Frankie on the screen, they knew they had found their Malcolm. They wanted Frankie Muniz so badly that they changed the character's age to fit the young actor. Now it was thumbs up all the way!

NEW JERSEY ROOTS

Frankie Muniz was born Francisco Muniz IV on December 5, 1985. Unlike Malcolm, Frankie is the baby of his family. There is no bullying older brother or sneaky younger brother as on "Malcolm in the Middle." Frankie and his older sister, Cristina, are very good friends.

The Muniz family lived in Woodridge, New Jersey, near Frankie's grandparents. When Frankie was five, his grandfather taught him to play golf. Golf quickly became Frankie's favorite sport. Frankie's grandfather must have been a great teacher. At fifteen years old, Frankie has an impressive 13 handicap. This means he plays golf at a level most adults would envy!

Frankie learned how to play golf, his favorite sport, from his grandfather.

The Muniz family moved to North Carolina when Frankie was eight. His mother, Denise, was a nurse. His father, Frank, was in the restaurant business. It was after the move that Frankie got bitten by the acting bug. His first audition was the result of sibling rivalry.

ACTING FOR ATTENTION

Cristina Muniz got a role in a local production of the musical *Joseph and the Amazing Technicolor Dreamcoat*. The Muniz family went to see her in the show. Frankie enjoyed watching Cristina onstage. He wanted to try acting himself. After all, he didn't want his sister to steal all the attention around the house.

Frankie jumped at the chance to audition for a production of *A Christmas Carol*. Frankie was nine and had never acted before. He had no singing or dancing experience, either. After his audition, he walked out of the building having earned the role of Tiny Tim. What had the director seen in this young boy? The ability to turn on the charm and act naturally. This isn't a simple thing to do. Actors study for years trying to look natural onstage. For Frankie, being onstage felt like being at home.

LAUNCHING A CAREER

Everyone needs some luck to succeed. Frankie's luck came during a day of rehearsals for *A Christmas Carol.* An agent sitting in the theater watched Frankie command the stage. Afterward, he asked Frankie if he could sign him to a contract. Frankie said yes, and soon began auditioning for roles in commercials.

At first he was nervous, but after many auditions it became fun. "I just go in there and act like myself," he said. Frankie shot more than twenty commercials in North Carolina and New York City.

During this time, he continued acting in regional plays. He had roles in *The Wizard of Oz, Our Town, Oklahoma!,* and *The Sound of Music.* Acting in all of these productions taught Frankie some valuable lessons. He was learning how to play different characters, and how to work with directors and other actors. At a young age, Frankie was becoming a veteran. People began to take notice of this young actor. Casting directors wanted him to try out for television and movie roles. Frankie now had the chance to make a career out of his love for acting.

Fun Fact

Frankie auditioned more than thirty times before getting his first role in a commercial.

As a child, Frankie acted in many plays and TV commercials.

CHAPTER TWO

BUSY ACTOR

"I actually went up to the director after I saw the pilot [for "Malcolm in the Middle"] *and said, 'I want to redo it.' I hated myself in it."*

—**Frankie in *Entertainment Weekly***

BALANCING ACT

Frankie was finding himself on a lot of airplanes bound for New York City and Los Angeles. These two cities held the most auditions for commercials, movies, and TV shows.

Even though Frankie enjoys being a kid, he gets a thrill out of dressing up in style from time to time.

Frankie's mother, Denise, is not just his traveling companion. She's also his tutor.

Denise Muniz traveled with her son for every audition and performance. She also helped Frankie with his schoolwork and was his constant companion. They became very close friends.

All of this acting and traveling was fun, but there was a price. Frankie couldn't attend his regular school while traveling across the country for auditions. He needed a tutor. Child actors have to be schooled during the weekdays when they work. Usually, young actors have tutors on the set who work with them 3 hours every day.

Frankie's mom understood the schooling problem. She wanted Frankie to have the best opportunity to become a star, though. She decided to quit nursing and become Frankie's full-time tutor. Frankie has been homeschooled since the sixth grade. Denise goes with Frankie wherever a movie or commercial shoot sends him, so that he doesn't fall behind in his schoolwork.

Each day, Frankie spends nearly 10 hours on the "Malcolm in the Middle" set. His shooting schedule allows plenty of time for being tutored. When Frankie finishes a scene, he slips away to an office. There, he studies with his mom for 20-minute periods. Balancing school and work is easy for Frankie. He loves to learn and is a whiz at algebra.

EARLY SUCCESS

In 1997, Frankie's hard work as an actor earned him a small role in the made-for-TV drama, *To Dance with Olivia*. This was his big chance to get noticed by Hollywood directors. Frankie and his mom went to Los Angeles for the shoot.

To Dance with Olivia also starred Oscar-winning actor Louis Gossett Jr. Frankie played a boy who is accidentally killed. "I get shot in the very beginning of that one," Frankie recalls. Though Frankie's role was small, he already knew the actor's creed: Don't turn down work.

Did you know?

Malcolm and his TV family don't have a last name! Linwood Boomer, the executive producer, forgot to come up with one.

Frankie starred with Bernadette Peters in
What the Deaf Man Heard. His touching performance
earned him two award nominations.

Frankie's next TV movie, *What the Deaf Man Heard,* tested his acting ability. Frankie played Sammy, a boy who becomes mute after his mother dies. Frankie got to act alongside the multi-talented Bernadette Peters. Frankie was nominated for the *Hollywood Reporter* Young Star Award and the Young Artist of Hollywood Award.

17

After that, Frankie got a part in his first motion picture. The movie was called *It Had to Be You*. Again, Frankie's role was small. But he took the part to further his career. The more that people saw him, the more he'd be in demand as an actor.

In 1998, Frankie got to work with one of his acting role models, Michael J. Fox (above).

LANDING GREAT ROLES

Besides movies, Frankie played parts on TV shows. He appeared in "Sabrina, the Teenage Witch" and "Silk Stalkings." In 1998, Frankie landed a role on "Spin City." He got to work alongside one of his favorite stars, Michael J. Fox. Fox had made the successful leap from child star to adult actor. Frankie carefully watched how Michael played his role. The star gave Frankie some acting tips. Frankie learned that hard work, fan appeal, and a good show could keep an actor working for many years.

Frankie was cast in two back-to-back episodes. "Spin City" is shot in New York City, so Frankie was able to spend time with his grandparents in New Jersey. After "Spin City," Frankie was cast in a second movie, *Lost and Found*. This was a comedy starring David Spade, of "Saturday Night Live" and "Just Shoot Me" fame.

All of the roles Frankie had played in the previous two years were about to pay off. Hollywood casting directors now knew Frankie by name. Best of all, Frankie looked young for his age. At thirteen, Frankie stood less than 5 feet tall. He could easily pass for someone younger. This made him a hot property in Hollywood. Older kids who played younger roles had an advantage. They could pay attention on the set longer than younger actors. They learned their lines quicker. They also didn't get tired as often.

Frankie's next chance at stardom came in the 1999 movie *My Dog Skip*. Frankie played Willie Morris, a boy who has few friends. "Then he gets a dog," Frankie explains, "and the dog really changes his life. He realizes how much he learns from the dog." Frankie's performance proved that he had everything that an actor needs to be a star. He was good-

Frankie holds his canine costar from *My Dog Skip*.

looking, he could play serious and comedic roles, and he was a natural actor. Critics praised Frankie. *My Dog Skip* made more than $30 million. Frankie was making a splash, but it was nothing compared to the success to come.

21

CHAPTER THREE

MALCOLM AND STARDOM

"I play all sports. I hang out with my friends, go to the movies. I go to the mall, just like normal people do. I'm normal."

—Frankie in *Teen Celebrity*

The Fox network planned on auditioning hundreds of kids for the lead role in "Malcolm in the Middle." Child actors from all across America answered the casting call. As it turned out, the producers did not have to look for long.

With its wacky scripts and talented cast, Frankie knew right away that "Malcolm in the Middle" would become a big hit.

The men from "Malcolm" pose for the cameras.

TIMING IS EVERYTHING

Frankie had dreamed of getting his own TV series ever since he started acting. For a thirteen-year-old, you might think that such an ambition would be *just* a dream. Frankie had other ideas, however. He was hard-working, and knew he was at the right age. Now he just needed the right show to make the dream come true.

Frankie had already appeared in two pilots. A pilot is a TV show's first episode. Network executives view the pilot, and then decide if they want to buy and produce the show. Frankie had acted in the pilots for "Claire's Kitchen" and "The Invisible Man," but the networks didn't buy either show. Of course, the "Malcolm" audition would not be Frankie's last chance. Yet Frankie knew that "Malcolm in the Middle" had everything he wanted. It was a sitcom based on a middle-class family. The characters were quirky, or weird. The script made Frankie laugh.

"Malcolm in the Middle" executive producer Linwood Boomer remembered the casting call. "On the second day of casting, we got a tape from New York, and Frankie was there," Linwood told *People*. Linwood said it was obvious that Frankie was perfect for the part. Of course, Frankie was sure he'd struck out. The producers had made it clear that the character would be nine years old. "I thought I was way too old," Frankie said. "A thirteen-year-old playing a nine-year-old?"

In Hollywood, however, there are always changes. The producers changed Malcolm's age to twelve. They phoned Frankie to tell him they wanted him to be their star. Frankie was in a Los Angeles hotel room when he got the call. He was so excited that he jumped wildly on the bed.

A PERFECT FAMILY

Quirky is one way of describing the "Malcolm in the Middle" characters. Let's just say they're very different from your average family. That's what drew Frankie to the role of Malcolm in the first place.

"There are TV families that are…perfect," Frankie observed. "[You might think,] 'Gosh, I wish my family was like that.'

Just like their TV characters, the cast of "Malcolm" likes to show off their wild and zany sides.

'Malcolm in the Middle' is more like, 'That's my family.'" Frankie does see the difference between his sitcom family and others. "I think maybe we go over the top just a little bit."

"Over the top" is a good way to put it. Does your mother shave your father's back hair in the kitchen? Has your brother been found to be a genius? How often does your mother throw out her back while yelling at you? Yes, this is Frankie's television family.

STARRING ROLE

Frankie worked very hard during his first days on the set. As the star, he was the center of attention. He acted in nearly every scene. Part of his role as

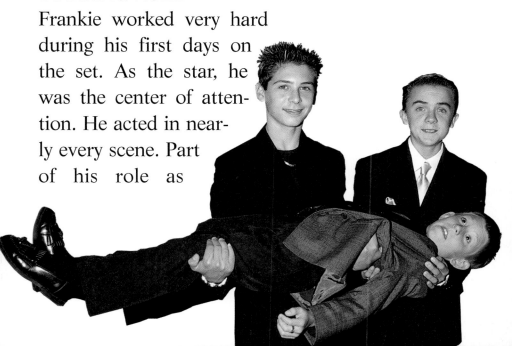

Malcolm was to interact with the TV audience. He had to speak directly to the camera.

Frankie recalled, "It was sort of weird, because you're usually told, 'Don't look at the camera.'" Breaking an old habit comes easily with good advice, though. The director told Frankie to treat the camera like a friend. Frankie imagined the camera was a buddy from New Jersey. That advice changed everything. "By the second time [we shot the scene], it came naturally."

MALCOLM MAKES HIS MARK

Fox planned to begin airing "Malcolm in the Middle" in September 1999. Frankie was thrilled. *My Dog Skip* would open in theaters the following January. Kids would already know his face by then. The lead-up to the premiere would help the movie do well.

At the last minute, Fox executives pushed

"Malcolm" to a January 2000 premiere. They did this because they were excited about the show and wanted more time to tell the press about it. Frankie wasn't happy with the change, but he understood. Fox producers used the extra time to promote the show. They ran a publicity campaign that put Frankie's face in newspapers and on magazine covers and billboards. Frankie even saw his face on the sides of buses going down the street! The extra effort paid off. Critics gave the show rave reviews. The sitcom debuted at number five in the ratings. It has been a big hit ever since.

Frankie was the talk of the town. As

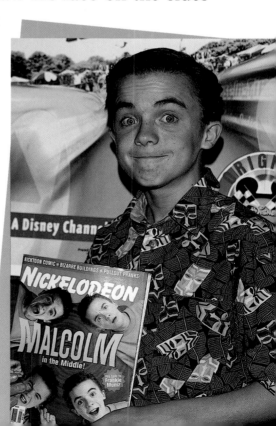

As his show's success grew by leaps and bounds, Frankie found his face popping up everywhere!

the star of a sitcom and the film *My Dog Skip*, he began making the rounds of talk shows. He appeared on "Live with Regis and Kathie Lee," "The Rosie O'Donnell Show," and "The Tonight Show with Jay Leno." Frankie introduced himself to America, and America fell in love with the blue-eyed teenager.

Frankie loves being interviewed. He knows it's part of the business. He says all actors should welcome the opportunity. He likes it most when he sees his face on the cover of magazines. "The best was seeing myself on the cover of *Super Teen*," Frankie told *USA Today*. "It was always a dream of mine to be in one of those publications."

FANS AND FRIENDS

Frankie knows that his fan base is kids. That's why he was thrilled to be nominated for a Nickelodeon Kids' Choice Award. He was even

Frankie always finds time to sign autographs for his devoted fans.

asked to co-host the awards show! Although he didn't win the award, he liked being part of the show. "It's kids voting," says Frankie, "not some academy of old people."

Frankie understands that many people want to be his friend only because he is a TV star. They don't really know who he is. That's one part of showbiz to which he's still adjusting. Frankie recently told *Teen Celebrity*, "Most fans just ask for a signed autograph. But then there are some girls who are like, 'I love you. I love your show!' It's so weird."

Frankie is wise beyond his years. He knows who his real friends are. "Kids want to be my friend now because I'm getting famous," he says. "I don't think they are my true friends." Frankie's New Jersey pals still treat him the same as before. They know Frankie doesn't want special treatment. He just wants to be a kid.

MIRACLES HAPPEN

Frankie received many movie offers during his first season playing Malcolm. He decided to star in *Miracle in Lane 2*. Frankie shot this Disney Channel movie during a summer hiatus, or break, from "Malcolm in the Middle." Frankie played Justin Holmes, a wheelchair-bound boy. Justin wants to play sports and win trophies. His chance comes when he enters a soapbox derby.

Frankie's part in *Miracle in Lane 2* made him appreciate his good fortune.

In this role, Frankie played a character who was based on a real person. It was a part that made Frankie think about how lucky he was. "I have to be really thankful that I'm not disabled," Frankie said. "But for [some handicapped people] to be so happy about their lives—you know, just happy with how they are—is so great!"

SILVER SCREEN

In April 2000, Frankie landed his next dramatic role. This time he was working with the famous director Martin Scorsese on *Deuces Wild*. Scorsese has directed hit movies like *Goodfellas* and *Casino*. For *Deuces Wild*, Scorsese was the executive producer. This film was different from Frankie's kid flicks. He played Scooch, a tough kid from Brooklyn. The film was set in Brooklyn in 1958.

CHAPTER FOUR

THE FUTURE FOR FRANKIE

"If you want to get into show business, you have to be ready to work hard and never give up."

—Frankie in *16* magazine

As the third season of "Malcolm in the Middle" begins, Frankie has many decisions to make. The fifteen-year-old TV and movie star already knows one thing for sure: He loves playing Malcolm and plans to stay on the show for its full TV run.

Frankie's fans have enjoyed watching the young star grow up before their eyes.

FOREVER YOUNG

After the first season, Bryan Cranston (who plays Malcolm's dad) feared Frankie would grow too quickly. Once he grew, his looks would change. Of course, that's not a bad thing. All kids change when they reach puberty. Frankie's change, however, would change the look and feel of the show. Cranston suggested that thirty-five episodes should be shot right away. That would be a way to capture Frankie as the short, cute kid he was in the pilot episode.

The producers said no. They wanted "Malcolm in the Middle" to grow and change around its child actors. The fans would grow with the show. It's a good thing the producers thought this. In the year between the pilot episode and the start of the second season, Frankie grew seven inches!

MALCOLM AND ME

With all his other opportunities, Frankie still loves playing Malcolm. The critics love him, too. In January 2001, Frankie received a Golden Globe nomination for Best Actor in a Comedy Series. In July 2001, he was nominated for an Emmy for Outstanding Lead Actor in a Comedy Series.

"Playing Malcolm is a lot of fun," Frankie recently told an online chat group. "The family part of it makes it even more fun. [Malcolm is] a kid that wants to be normal."

STILL A KID

Frankie may be growing up, but he still loves to entertain kids. Frankie says he wants to attract a following for as long as possible. Recently, Frankie told *MSN* magazine that he might do another project with Disney. It is a

Did you know?

Frankie already has experience playing an animated character. He did a voice-over on an episode of Fox's biggest hit, "The Simpsons."

cartoon titled *Meatball Finkelstein,* and Frankie would do the voice of a cartoon character.

Frankie knows it will be difficult to grow from kid actor to adult star. Few child actors have made this career change. His role models include Michael J. Fox, Matt Dillon, and Jodie Foster. Right now, Frankie is happy with being a teen. The key to Frankie's happiness is the fun he has while acting. If acting stops being fun for him, he says he will quit. He loves to work, and gets bored when he's not working.

Frankie plans to go to college. He knows

With a hit show and a bright future ahead of him, Frankie certainly has his hands full.

how important an education is to a person's life. And then what? Even though Frankie is living his dream right now, he has others. He wants to play professional golf, be part of the Blue Man Group, and own the Los Angeles Clippers basketball team. "Those are my back-ups," Frankie says. Hey, why not? Malcolm may be in the middle—but Frankie Muniz is on top!

TIMELINE

1985 • Frankie is born in Woodridge, New Jersey.

1993 • Frankie moves with his family to Raleigh, North Carolina.

1994 • Frankie plays the part of Tiny Tim in a production of *A Christmas Carol.*
• Frankie signs with a talent agent and begins acting in TV commercials.

1994–1996 • Frankie continues his stage acting with roles in *The Wizard of Oz, Our Town, Oklahoma!,* and *The Sound of Music.*

1997 • Frankie appears in the TV movies *To Dance with Olivia* and *What the Deaf Man Heard.*

1998 • Frankie lands his first motion picture role as Franklin in *It Had to Be You.*

TIMELINE

1998
- Frankie appears on TV shows such as "Spin City," "Sabrina, the Teenage Witch," and "Silk Stalkings."

1999
- Frankie is cast in another motion picture, *Lost and Found*.
- Frankie auditions for the starring role of "Malcolm in the Middle" and earns the role over hundreds of other child actors.

2000
- Frankie is the star of his next motion picture release, *My Dog Skip*.
- Frankie is nominated for a Nickelodeon Kids' Choice Award.
- Frankie stars as Justin in *Miracle in Lane 2*.

2001
- Frankie is nominated for a Golden Globe.
- Frankie stars in the film *Deuces Wild*.
- Frankie receives an Emmy nomination for Outstanding Lead Actor in a Comedy Series.

FACT SHEET

Name	Francisco James Muniz IV
Nickname	Frankie
Born	December 5, 1985
Birthplace	Woodridge, New Jersey
Family	Mother: Denise; Father: Frank; Sister: Cristina
Sign	Sagittarius
Height	5'7"
Hair	Brown
Eyes	Blue
Pets	Cat (Pumpkin), dog (Cadillac)
Car	He will be eligible to drive on December 5, 2001; Frankie wants to buy a Cadillac Escalade

Favorites

Food	Hamburgers and french fries
Candy	Snickers bars
Actors	Michael J. Fox, Val Kilmer, and Leonardo DiCaprio
Subjects	Geography and algebra
Music	"Anything except rap"
Team	L.A. Clippers (basketball)
Sports	Golf, baseball, basketball, and skateboarding
Book	*Dragonwings* by Lawrence Yep

NEW WORDS

agent a person who finds jobs for actors, models, and musicians

audition a tryout performance in hopes of getting a role in a movie or TV show

commercial an advertisement that airs on television or radio

critics people who review movies, TV shows, or plays

director the person in charge of filming a movie or TV show

hiatus when the cast and crew of a TV show take a break, usually in the summer

homeschooled to be taught or tutored at home, often by a parent

mute unable to speak

nomination the selection of someone to compete for an award

pilot the first episode of a new series

NEW WORDS

producer the person who supervises and raises money for a film or TV show

quirky weird; having a strange but lovable personality

regional of or in a particular area; local

role a part played by an actor in a movie, TV show, or play

sitcom a TV comedy series; episodes are usually thirty minutes long

veteran someone with a lot of experience

FOR FURTHER READING

Krulik, Nancy. *Frankie Muniz: Boy Genius.* New York: Archway, 2000.

Levithan, David. *Malcolm in the Middle: My Class Project* (fiction). New York: Scholastic, 2000.

Mason, Tom. *Malcolm in the Middle: Life Is Unfair* (fiction). New York: Scholastic, 2000.

RESOURCES

WEB SITES

The Official "Malcolm in the Middle" Web Site
www.fox.com/malcolminthemiddle/
Learn more about Malcolm's family and friends on this site. You can also read Malcolm's journal.

Frankie Muniz!
www.expage.com/Frankiemunizfanatics
This site has many facts about Frankie and links to other Frankie sites.

MunizMania
munizmania.tripod.com
Read all about Frankie and Malcolm on this site. There are also interviews, a photo gallery, and links to other sites about Frankie.

You can send an e-mail to Frankie at: Munizmania@tripod.com

INDEX

INDEX

ABOUT THE AUTHOR

Mark Beyer is a freelance writer living in Florida. He has written dozens of books for young readers.